Mara and Friends 1

Storybook

Improving Reading Skills For
Children 4 - 5 Years Old

Claire Mark

ISBN # 9798668806713

CONTENTS

Get the Ball, Sassy!

Mum takes Mara, Ash and their dog Sassy to the park. Mum looks on as they play. Ash likes the slide. Mara plays 'Get the Ball' with Sassy and meets two new friends, Vishnu and Indra. Find out how Indra becomes a special friend!

In this story you will meet:

Mum, mother of **Mara** and little brother, **Ash**.

Friends, **Vishnu** and little sister, **Indra**.

Sassy, Mara's dog.

A Visit to the Park

We are in the park.

Here we can jump!

Here we can run!

We go on the slide.

It is fun, fun, fun!

One, two, three,

Mara, look at me!

I can go up!

I can go down!

Mum, did Mara see?

MARA AND SASSY PLAY   1

Mara and Sassy are at the

park.

Sit Sassy, sit.

Sassy sits.

Mara pats Sassy.

Mara and Sassy sit in the park.

Mara plays in the park.

Sassy plays in the park.

Play Mara. Play Sassy.

Sassy runs to get to Mara.

Mara and Sassy play.

MARA AND SASSY PLAY 2

Mara had a red and yellow ball. Mara hops in the park. Mara hops and plays.

Sassy plays. Mara and Sassy play in the park.

Run for the ball, Sassy, said Mara. Sassy runs for the ball,

Sassy gets the ball and runs to Mara.

MARA AND SASSY PLAY 3

Run for the ball, Sassy, said

Mara. Sassy runs for the ball,

but Sassy did not get the ball.

Where is the ball? Where is

the ball?

Mara cannot see it.

Sassy cannot see it. Where is the red and yellow ball?

Mara and Sassy cannot find it.

AT THE SLIDE 1

Mara and Sassy look for the ball.

They get to the slide.

Mum is at the slide.

Mara runs to Mum. Mara hugs Mum.

Ash is at the slide.

Mara sees Ash go up
the steps.

Ash sees Mara and Sassy.

Ash said, Hello Mara!

AT THE SLIDE 2

Mum hugs Mara.

Look Mara! Ash is on the

slide, said Mum.

Yes, it is fun, said Mara.

Mara, look at me!

Look at me! said Ash.

One, two, three! said Ash.

Mara sees Ash go down the slide!

Mara and Sassy did not find the ball at the slide.

SASSY WANTS TO PLAY TAG 1

Mara and Sassy look for
the red and yellow ball.

We can find the ball Sassy,
said Mara.

Mara sees two girls and three boys.

The girls ran!
The boys ran!

The girls and boys play tag in the park.

SASSY WANTS TO PLAY TAG 2

Sassy looks at the girls and boys. They play tag. It is fun!

Sassy jumps on Mara.

Down Sassy, down! said Mara. Let us look for the red and yellow ball.

Mara and Sassy look for the ball.

But Mara and Sassy did not find the red and yellow ball here.

AT THE SWINGS

Sassy sees a little girl in a blue dress. She is on a swing.

The little girl is Indra. She is with Vishnu. The swings go up and down. It is fun!

The little girl looks at Sassy.

Sassy wags, wags, wags!

Hello dog! said the little girl.

Sassy sits and looks at Indra.

Mara looks for the ball but she did not find it at the swings.

MARA IS SAD 1

I am sad, said Mara.

She sits on a bench in the park.

Vishnu and Indra see Mara.

They sit on the bench.

Hello! I am Indra, and this is my big brother, Vishnu, said Indra.

Vishnu, Indra and Mara shake hands.

Mara said, Hello! I am Mara, and this is my dog, Sassy.

MARA IS SAD 2

Vishnu pats Sassy.

Indra looks at the dog.
Come Sassy! said Indra.

Sassy! Do not go away,
said Vishnu.

Come here Sassy! said Indra.

Sassy runs to Indra.

Indra pats Sassy.

Sassy, said Vishnu, you are
a funny dog.

You look sad, Mara, said Vishnu.

Yes, I am a bit sad, said Mara.

I cannot find my red and
yellow ball. It makes me sad.

We can help you to find the red
and yellow ball Mara, said Vishnu.

Mara, Vishnu, Indra and

Sassy look for the red
and yellow ball.

Vishnu and Indra help Mara. Indra and Sassy look for the ball on a bench in the park.

Vishnu looks for the ball under a bench in the park.

They look and look and look.
Sassy finds a little red ball.

Sassy, said Vishnu, you are
funny! You did not find the
red and yellow ball.

INDRA, SASSY AND A BIG BIN 1

Come Sassy. Please find the ball for me! said Indra.

Sassy runs to Indra.

Indra and Sassy look and look for the ball.

Sassy sees a big bin. Sassy runs to the bin. Sassy finds the red and yellow ball!

Indra hugs Sassy.

Indra is happy! Sassy is happy!

INDRA, SASSY AND A BIG BIN 2

Look Mara, said Vishnu,

Indra and Sassy got the

ball.

Indra and Sassy got the ball!

Mara is happy.

Sassy runs to Mara.

Mara gets the red and yellow

ball!

Thank you, Indra!

Good dog, Sassy! said Mara.

I got my red and yellow ball

and I got two friends,

Indra and Vishnu!

Review

vc and cvc Words/ Sight Words

Units

1. at sit pat in run get / and the in play run to
   had red hop / a red yellow for said
   but did not it /not where is can see it find
2. Mum hug up / look go up
   on yes fun / me one two three down
3. tag / we
   let us / jump here
4. in wag dog / little blue
5. am sad / I my big
   pat / come away you funny
6. bit can / make help
   - / under
7. big bin / please
   got / good

Units   Reading Comprehension

1. Where were Mum, Mara and Ash?

   What game did Mara and Sassy play with the ball?

   What was the colour of Mara's ball?

   Why were they unable to continue with their ball game?

   What did Mara then decide to do?

2. Where was Ash? Was he having fun? Why
   did Mara not stay and play with him?

3. Mara sees some happy boys and girls. What is the name
   of the game that they played? How is this game played?

4. Where in the park did Mara first meet Vishnu and
   Indra? How did Sassy show that she liked Indra?

5. How did Vishnu, Indra and Mara introduce themselves
   when they met again? Vishnu and Indra decided to help
   Mara. How do you think Mara felt when her new friends
   offered to help her find the ball?

6. What was the colour of the first ball that Sassy found?

7. Indra and Sassy got the ball. Where was it found?
   Please and **Thank-You** are very special words. When
   were they used during the story? If Mara had been
   impolite to Vishnu and Indra, how do you think the
   story could have ended?

Reading Comprehension exercises: *Questions are read by the teacher/parent, and children respond orally.* These discussions help the child to make personal connections with what has been read in the story.

On successful completion of reading *Get The Ball, Sassy!* **(Mara and Friends 1 Storybook),** the child should be able to:

- demonstrate increased knowledge of single letter sounds and associate them with symbols
- relate consonant and short vowel sounds to letters of the alphabet
- listen for and identify initial, medial and final sounds in **cvc** (consonant/vowel/consonant) words in correct left to right order
- blend letter sounds to decode simple **cvc** words for reading, using knowledge of phonemes (spoken letter sounds) and graphemes (written letter unit or units representing a sound)
- recognize appropriately levelled *Pre-K Dolch Sight Words and some frequently used words
- recognize use of punctuation: full stops, commas, question marks and exclamation marks
- recognize use of capital letters
- demonstrate awareness of inflectional ending **'s'** to some root words (without change in root word)
- read stories that contain levelled Sight Word vocabulary, decodable **cvc** words and familiar words that are decodable by using context and picture clues
- listen and respond eagerly and attentively to stories and participate actively in class discussions
- retell a story, identifying the main character and relating the sequence of events

* Edward William Dolch, Ph.D (1889-1961), author of children's stories and texts, first published the Dolch Word List in a journal article in 1936. He then published it in his book 'Problems in Reading' in 1948. The Dolch Sight Words have assisted many children to enjoy reading

About the Author

Mrs. Claire Mark, a retired schoolteacher, taught at Primary and Secondary levels for close to 40 years. She obtained outstanding results on completion of a formal course in the Teaching of Reading offered at the UWI School of Continuing Studies. This served to enhance her skills in this field, thus sparking her interest to produce appropriate and stimulating material for some of her adolescent students. On retirement she continued to assist even younger children, writing stories and rhymes that included levelled phonics, sight-words and situations to encourage active class discussion. This made the reading experience meaningful and enjoyable. These books are a result of evolving interest over the years in promoting early literacy and good citizenship in children.

CPSIA information can be obtained
at www.ICGtesting.com
Printed in the USA
BVRC090601301121
622807BV00031B/31